Keys to Understanding the Bible

by Jarrod Jacobs

© 2017 One Stone Press.
All rights reserved. No part of this book may be reproduced
in any form without written permission of the publisher.

Published by:
One Stone Press
979 Lovers Lane
Bowling Green, KY 42103

Printed in the United States of America

ISBN 10: 1-941422-22-5
ISBN 13: 978-1-941422-22-9

Supplemental Materials Available:
Answer key
Downloadable PDF

www.onestone.com

Introduction

The book you have in your hands is intended for those who are new to the faith and for those who wish to reinforce their faith. It can be used as a personal study or in a class setting. This book is simple in some ways, but hopefully it contains several challenging aspects to those who read and study its pages. Make sure to study this book with Bible in hand: You will need it!

At the end of each chapter, there is a series of questions. Some of these challenge you in the area of memory work and some challenge you with your knowledge of the lesson. As the questions continue, the degree of difficulty increases. Try to challenge yourself as you study this book and answer every question in each chapter.

May God bless you in your study.

- Jarrod Jacobs

Table of Contents

1. Keys to Bible Comprehension 7
2. Keys to Bible Reading 11
3. Keys to Bible Study 15
4. Keys to Proper Division in the Bible (Part 1) 21
5. Keys to Proper Division in the Bible (Part 2) 27
6. Keys to a Good Prayer Life 31
7. Keynotes of Scripture (Part 1) 35
8. Keynotes of Scripture (Part 2) 39
9. Keynotes of Scripture (Part 3) 43

Lesson 1

Keys to Bible Comprehension

INTRODUCTION

I. MEMORY VERSE: **Psalm 119:11**

II. This series of lessons takes you through some basics of Bible study and application.

   A. God says the blessed man is the one who _____ in God's word **(Psalm 1:2)**.

      1. To meditate is to endeavor to understand its meaning; he has pleasure in reflecting on it. It is not a subject which he puts away from him, or in respect to which he is indifferent, but he keeps it before his mind and has satisfaction in doing it (*Barnes' Notes - Psalms*, p. 4).

      2. The same word was used when God spoke to Joshua. "You shall _____ in it day and night…" **(Joshua 1:8)**.

      3. Paul stated a similar thing when writing to Timothy. "_____ on these things; give yourself entirely to them, that your progress may be evident to all" **(1 Timothy 4:15)**.

   B. If we are going to be what God wants us to be, we *can not* ignore His word! We must spend time in meditation and study of His word.

III. The purpose of this study is to:

   A. Give us a better understanding of the general makeup of the Bible (ex: books of Bible; divisions in the Bible, etc.)

   B. Teach us how to read the Bible

   C. Teach us how to study the Bible (There is a difference between reading and studying!)

   D. Teach us the theme of the Bible

   E. Teach us the importance and necessity of memory work

   F. Acquaint us with many of the principal people in the Bible.

DISCUSSION

I. You can trust the Bible!

   A. One thing we must understand is that the Bible can be trusted. It is:

      1. Eternal **(Psalm 117:2, 100:5, 119:89; Matthew 24:35; 1 Peter 1:25)**

      2. Practical **(Proverbs; James; etc.)**

      3. Moral **(Matthew 7:12)**

      4. Truth **(John 17:17)**

      5. Righteous **(Psalm 119:172; Romans 1:16-17)**

   B. The Bible is the standard by which man will be judged one day **(John 12:48)**.

   C. The Bible displays a continuity that no other book has. Can you imagine trying to get a group of only 4 or 5 men to write something on which all were agreed?

      1. In order to best accomplish your goal, what might you need to do?

      2. Think about this: The Bible was written over a span of 1,600 years (60+ generations) by 40 authors from every walk of life!

      3. Name some Biblical writers and their occupations: _____
         _____
         _____

      4. The Bible was written on 3 continents (Asia, Africa, Europe).

      5. The Bible was also written in three languages.

         a. Hebrew: the language of the Old Testament (**2 Kings 18:26-28**, language of the Jews/Judah; **Isaiah 19:18**, language of Canaan)

         b. Aramaic: the *lingua franca* (language widely used as a means of communication among speakers of other languages—*Webster's*) during the time of Alexander the Great (6th century B.C. to 4th century B.C.)

         c. Greek: the international language during the time of Christ and the New Testament

   D. Yet, within the Bible we find no flaws, no errors, etc. The claims and statements of the Bible have been proven true again and again through the years!

LESSON 1 Keys to Bible Comprehension 9

II. The major divisions found in the Bible:

 A. In order to better appreciate the Bible, we need to familiarize ourselves with certain facts.

 1. How many books are found in the Bible? _____

 2. Can you name all of the books in the Bible? _____
 (If not, during this series of lessons, we will learn them.)

 B. Furthermore, the books of the Bible can be categorized in the following way:

 1. Old Testament

 a. Books of Law (Pentateuch) _____
 _____

 b. Books of History _____
 _____
 _____

 c. Books of Wisdom _____
 _____

 d. Major Prophets _____
 _____

 e. Minor Prophets _____
 _____
 _____

 f. It may help to know these books can be divided into groups as follows: 5-12-5-5-12

 2. New Testament

 a. Record of the life of Christ (Gospel) _____

 b. History of the church _____

 c. Epistles _____
 _____
 _____

 d. Prophecy _____

III. The theme of the Bible:

   A. From the time of **Genesis 3** to the end of the Bible, the theme of the Bible is _____

   B. From the Old Testament to the New Testament, we see the unfolding of God's plan of salvation.

      1. God's plan for salvation was fulfilled through the family of _____.

      2. Specifically, our Savior came from the tribe of _____.

      3. Because of the _____, _____, and _____ of Christ, men can be saved today **(Romans 6:3-5, 17-18)**.

   C. Christ is the central figure of the Bible; all the Old Testament faith heroes pointed to Him, and all the New Testament characters pointed back to Him.

   D. Redemption is the central event of the Bible. If not for this, man would have no chance of going to Heaven when this life is over.

ASSIGNMENTS

(Hint: Assignments increase in difficulty. While you may not be able to answer each question, please challenge yourself and do the best you can!)

1. Do you know the books of the Bible? If not, memorize the first 10 books for our next class.

2. If you know the books of the Bible, then be prepared to discuss the divisions of the Bible.

3. Memorize the 15 judges and God's purpose for raising up judges.

4. Paul names the *where, to whom, what,* and *how* of salvation (the theme of the Bible) in **Ephesians 2:13, 16**. Read those verses and explain the *where, to whom, what,* and *how* of salvation. _____
_____
_____
_____
_____

Lesson 2

Keys to Bible Reading

INTRODUCTION

I. MEMORY VERSE: **Psalm 119:18**

II. Much of the religious division seen today is based upon misconceptions when reading the Bible.

   A. Some problems:

   1. Reading to prove your point **(Matthew 4:6)**.

   2. Reading with prejudice **(John 7:40-44)**.

   3. Reading with little or no comprehension **(Acts 8:30-31, 34)**.

   4. Reading about God's word rather than spending time reading God's word.

   B. This lesson encourages us to read the Bible and comprehend what we read!

DISCUSSION

I. The importance of the written word

   A. God places a premium on the written word!

   1. Jesus asked, "Have ye not _____" no less than seven times in the New Testament **(Matthew 12:3, 5, 19:4, 22:31; Mark 12:10, 26; Luke 6:3)**.

   B. The advantages of the printed page

   1. There are opportunities to reread something one does not understand.

   2. The printed page is of an abiding nature, where the spoken word is often filtered and reinterpreted when repeated.

   3. The printed page continues to teach future generations long after the author has died.

   4. The Bible teaches us new things each time we read those familiar passages.

C. There are many advantages to the printed page, especially when one considers that the Bible contains God's instructions on how to reach Heaven!

II. God encourages the reading of His word

A. Perhaps the most obvious example of this is **Psalm 119**. Each verse in this psalm glorifies the written word in some way!

1. Read **Psalm 119** and notice how David mentions the word of God in every passage. He does so by using such terms as: _____ _____

2. David recognized the reason he had wisdom was because of God's word **(Psalm 119:98-100)**.

B. Paul was a believer in the written word, telling Timothy: "Till I come, give attendance to _____, to _____, to _____ **(1 Timothy 4:13)**."

C. Paul wrote the _____ brethren, and told them, "Whereby, when ye _____, ye may _____ my _____ in the mystery of _____ **(Ephesians 3:4)**."

III. Suggestions for successful Bible reading

A. Read passages more than once.

1. Sometimes, it is after reading a passage three or four times that we begin to see the flow of thought and purpose behind what was written.

2. God expected the kings of His people to read the Scripture and then write it down daily **(Deuteronomy 17:18-20)**.

3. This would be a good habit for "kings and priests" today **(Revelation 1:5-6; 1 Peter 2:9)**.

B. Read the passage aloud.

1. Did you know that the Bible was written in such a way as to be read aloud **(Nehemiah 8:1-3)**?

2. While our society practices silent reading, it used to not be this way **(Acts 8:30)**. Read the passages below and note what God told Moses, Joshua, and Paul to do.

a. **Exodus 24:7** _____

b. **Deuteronomy 31:10-12** _____

c. **Joshua 8:35** _____

d. **1 Thessalonians 5:27** _____

e. **Colossians 4:16** _____

STATISTICS ON BIBLE READING TIME

It takes an average of 70 hours and 40 minutes to read the Bible aloud. This breaks down as follows:

- 52 hours and 20 minutes is the average time required to read the Old Testament.
- 18 hours and 20 minutes is the average time required to read the New Testament.
- The book of Psalms takes the longest to read, at 4 hours and 28 minutes.
- The book of Luke takes about 2 hours and 43 minutes to read.

Don't forget: There are **24** hours in a day, **168** hours in a week, and **8,760** hours in a year. Therefore, don't allow a systematic Bible reading schedule to intimidate you!

---

3. When we combine the senses of sight and hearing, it helps us comprehend what we are reading.

    a. Hearing the words spoken helps us catch the tone in what is being said.

    b. Therefore, don't feel afraid or self-conscious about reading aloud!

READING EXERCISE

Do you notice anything wrong with this this sentence?

C. Read often.

   1. God's word is often compared to spiritual food **(1 Peter 2:2; Hebrews 5:12-14)**.

   2. Therefore, to neglect the reading of God's word is equivalent to starving the soul!

   3. How much time do we spend reading God's word on a daily basis? Weekly basis? This is our spiritual food. Is it right to starve the soul?

   D. Respect the silence of the Scriptures!

   1. Be careful to let the Scriptures speak, and do not read into the text something that is not there.

      a. Example: People read of a household being saved **(Acts 16:15)**, and assume this includes babies!

      b. Example: People read of the birth of Christ and assume that He wants special religious celebrations held in honor of His birth.

   2. Let us be satisfied to simply read God's word as is and be silent when God is silent!

ASSIGNMENTS

(Hint: Assignments increase in difficulty. While you may not be able to answer each question, please challenge yourself and do the best you can!)

1. Do you know the books of the Bible? (You should know **Genesis—2 Samuel**. Memorize the next 10 books of the Bible.)

2. Memorize the 12 sons of Israel and 12 (original) apostles. Who were the two added to the apostles in the book of Acts?

3. In this lesson, we referred to the words of Moses and Christ. What comparisons can be made? _____
_____
_____
_____

Lesson 3

Keys to Bible Study

INTRODUCTION

I. MEMORY VERSE: **Acts 17:11**

II. Why encourage people to study the Bible?

   A. This is an expedient way to obtain a thorough knowledge of the word of God.

   B. Studying helps one "rightly divide" (handle accurately and correctly) God's word **(2 Timothy 2:15)**.

   C. Reading, in contrast to studying, requires different methods and degrees of effort.

   1. Read: to peruse and apprehend the meaning of (something written, printed, etc.) (*Webster's*).

   2. Study: application of the mind to the acquisition (gaining possession) of knowledge, as by reading, investigation, or reflection (ibid.)

      a. The Biblical word for study is the word "meditation." We find this word in: **Psalm 1:2** and **1 Timothy 4:15** ("Take pains with these things; be absorbed in them...", NAS)

      b. While reading is involved in studying, when one reads, he is not necessarily studying!

      c. Some helps to get you started in a methodical study of God's word: *A Guide To Bible Study* by J.W. McGarvey; *How To Study The Bible* by R.A. Torrey; *Guide To Bible Study* by James Tolle; *Effective Bible Study* by Howard Vos.

   D. Studying God's will means making a concentrated effort to learn His will more perfectly!

III. For many, the question boils down to this basic question: "How do I study God's word?"

IV. This lesson focuses on some basic rules for effective Bible study.

16 Keys to Understanding the Bible

DISCUSSION

I. Observe who speaks

  A. Yes, this is an elementary point, but many fail to do this, and confusion is the result!

  B. It is very important to know who is speaking in the passage being studied. Why?

   1. Because some are lying (name some): _____
   _____

   2. Because some are teaching valuable lessons to be applied to self. Read the following verses and state who is speaking and what lesson can be learned today:

      a. **Mark 16:16** _____
      _____

      b. **Philippians 4:8** _____
      _____

      c. **1 Thessalonians 5:17** _____
      _____

      d. **1 John 5:2-3** _____
      _____

      e. **Jude 3** _____
      _____

   3. Because some speak from arrogance or a haughty mind: Read the following verses and note who is speaking and their attitude:

      a. **Daniel 4:30** _____
      _____

      b. **Luke 18:10-14** _____
      _____

   4. Because some speak from humility (name some):_____
   _____

  C. When we discern between the words of Satan, Paul, Christ, an angel, the publicans, the Pharisees, etc., we'll be on our way to a better understanding of the Bible.

LESSON 3 Keys to Bible Study   17

II. Observe to whom a command is given (and why)

   A. Some things are commanded in the Bible but are not expected to be obeyed today.

   1. Who is given the command and why?

      a. **Genesis 6:4** _____
         _____

      b. **John 2:7** _____
         _____

      c. **Joshua 6:2-5** _____
         _____

   2. At the same time, there are commands we must obey today. Read the verses below and explain who is to obey this command and why.

      a. **Ephesians 6:1-4** _____
         _____

      b. **Romans 13:1-2** _____
         _____

      c. **1 Thessalonians 5:17-18, 21-22** _____
         _____

      d. **1 Corinthians 11:24-25** _____
         _____

   B. When we study the Bible, such observations are important so that we do not jump to the wrong conclusion!

III. Study the context (setting)

   A. This is key to determining whether or not one handles God's word accurately **(2 Timothy 2:15)**.

   B. Context: the parts of a written or spoken statement that precede or follow a specific word or passage, usually influencing its meaning or effect (*Webster's*).

> **NOTE**
> - Chapter and verse divisions were not originally in the Bible. Stephen Langton in the 12th century added chapter divisions into the Latin Vulgate. Robert Estienne added verse divisions in 1551. The first Bible version to have verse divisions was the Geneva Bible (1560).
> - I note this here so that we understand chapter and verse divisions were added by men, and sometimes these divisions were poorly selected.
> - While chapter and verse divisions can be handy in finding a specific sentence or thought, it is not always helpful when determining context.

1. In studying the context of a Bible passage, you must read the verses before and after the one you are studying to appreciate the setting. At times, in order to understand the context, you may have to read the paragraph, chapter, or the entire book to truly grasp the context.

2. Many times, just reading one or two extra verses throws a whole new light on the subject. For example:

    a. Read **John 6:44**. How does God "draw" people to Him? _____

    Now read **verse 45**. How are we drawn to God? _____

    b. Read **Galatians 3:26**. Do we become God's children by faith only? _____

    Now read **verse 27**. What is necessary for being a child of God? _____

    c. Read **Romans 10:13**. How does one "call upon the name of the Lord?" _____

    Now read **verses 14-16**. You will now have the answer to this question! _____

C. If we ever wish to know God's word completely and apply it accurately, we need to understand the context of the passage.

LESSON 3 Keys to Bible Study   19

IV. Under which dispensation are we reading?

   A. Dispensation: a divinely appointed order or age (*Webster's*)

   B. There are three dispensations (ages, periods of time) in the Bible:

   1. The Patriarchal age, lasting roughly 2,500 years (From Adam to Moses)

   2. The Mosaic age, lasting roughly 1,500 years (From Moses to the cross)

   3. The Christian age, beginning after Christ's crucifixion to the end of time. At times, the Bible refers to this time period as "the last days" **(Isaiah 2:2; Joel 2:28; Acts 2:16-17; Hebrews 1:2)**.

   4. **Hebrews 1:1** says God spoke in various means/ways to the people. Examples: _____

   5. When we determine the dispensation in the Bible, we can know whether we are reading commands and examples applicable to us today or valuable lessons presented for us to gain knowledge **(Romans 15:4)**.

   C. If there is not a careful understanding of the dispensation in the Bible, we can confuse ourselves! Therefore, let us read the following verses and determine the dispensation.

   1. Noah built an ark **(Genesis 6:14-17, 22)** _____

   2. David used mechanical instruments **(Psalm 81:4; 2 Chronicles 29:25)** _____

   3. **Acts 2:42** _____

   D. When we study the Bible, let us respect the dispensations of time that are recorded here and make applications accordingly.

V. Use good common sense

   A. Reading a verse or chapter and hoping to understand it all takes time and effort. In fact, anything worthwhile takes time and effort **(Ecclesiastes 12:12)**.

   B. When studying the Bible, please notice:

   1. Who is the author or who is speaking?

      a. At times, the answer to this question is obvious. Yet, there are some books where the answer is not obvious.

b. Sometimes we won't know the earthly author of the book, but we know the One behind it is _____.

2. What topics are addressed?

3. Was God pleased or displeased with the people in the portion being read?

4. Is this an Old Testament book or a New Testament book?

5. The other rules we studied above.

C. We need to understand that what we study and what we learn must be in harmony with all of the Bible. This shows good common sense.

1. A good way to study is to work on the easier things and then study the harder passages in light of what we already know to be true.

2. The Bible is its own best commentary; use it!

a. Study by finding everything the Bible says on a subject, then read and accept it!

b. Read the Old Testament in light of the New, and vice versa.

ASSIGNMENTS

(Hint: Assignments increase in difficulty. While you may not be able to answer each question, please challenge yourself and do the best you can!)

1. Do you know the books of the Bible? (You should know **Genesis—Proverbs**. Memorize the next 10 books of the Bible.)

2. Do you know the judges? Do you know the sons of Israel?

3. Use the rules of study (Point V, B) to study the following: **Matthew 16:18; Acts 2:38; Genesis 6:14; Psalm 117; Jeremiah 6:15-16; Hebrews 8**

Lesson 4

Keys to Proper Division in the Bible (Part 1)

INTRODUCTION

I. MEMORY VERSE: **Romans 15:4; John 5:39**

II. As we apply the rules of proper reading and proper study to our Bible work from previous lessons, certain aspects should stand out in our minds. Among these are:

   A. Key families mentioned in the Bible.

   B. Key individuals noted by God.

III. These historical people may be in the Bible (Old or New Testament) for any number of reasons, but behind it all, their mention helps to develop the Bible's theme of _____.

IV. While an obvious figure mentioned in the Bible is Jesus the Christ, this lesson focuses on other key figures. Jesus Christ is the focus of the next lesson!

DISCUSSION

I. Adam and Eve

   A. What position do these two people hold in the Bible? _____

   B. There are many good things we can say about this first couple. However, these two have the dubious honor of being responsible for _____ **(Genesis 2:15-17, 3:3-6, 16-19)**.

   C. Though our next lesson focuses on Christ, we would be remiss if we did not mention that in the midst of the tragedy of the sin Adam and Eve committed, God promised _____ **(Genesis 3:15)**.

   D. Paul describes Adam as the first Adam **(1 Corinthians 15:45-48)**. Who is the last or second Adam? _____

22 Keys to Understanding the Bible

II. Noah

    A. The account of Noah's life is found in _____

        1. Who is Noah's father? Who is his grandfather? _____
        _____

        2. Name Noah's children. _____

    B. What great character trait does Noah possess? _____

        1. He is only one of two Bible characters specifically noted for walking with God **(Genesis 6:9)**.

        2. Name the other Bible character so described. _____

    C. Besides being the builder of the ark, Noah is described by Peter as being _____ **(2 Peter 2:5)**.

III. Abraham and Sarah

    A. Before he was known as Abraham, he was called _____

        1. What does that name mean? _____

        2. What does Abraham mean? _____

    B. Abraham is a father to _____ and a great-grandfather to _____

    C. It is said three times in the Bible that Abraham was God's _____ (_____; _____; **James 2:23**).

    D. Abraham and Sarah hold a special place in the Bible, for those who are Christians are not only considered children of God **(Romans 8:16-17)**, but also Abraham's _____ **(Galatians 3:29)** and Sarah's daughters **(1 Peter _____)**.

    E. Saying that Christians are children of Abraham and Sarah fulfills what prophecy? _____

IV. Moses

    A. Moses came from the tribe of _____, Abraham's great-grandson.

    B. He led the _____ out of _____, and finally to _____. (See: **Exodus-Deuteronomy**)

    C. Like Abraham, he was called God's _____ **(Exodus 33:11)**.

D. Moses was considered the great leader of God's people, and a type of
_____.

V. The prophets

A. Familiarize yourself with the prophets found in the Bible. (You should be aware of several prophets already, based upon our memorization of the books of the Bible.)

1. The word prophet literally means mouth. Those called prophets were considered the mouth of God. Why is this? _____

2. While, in a very real sense, we could say such men as Enoch, Noah, and others were prophets because they spoke God's word, usually we think of prophets as being people like _____.

B. These prophets had a responsibility to call people back to God. Once the Israelites had a king, we see that prophet and king are linked together by God. In the chart below, name the king(s) that would have been associated with the following prophet(s). (Note: There will be some overlap.)

Elijah (1 Kings 17—2 Kings 2)	Associated with:	King(s):
Jeremiah (Jeremiah)	Associated with:	King(s):
Micaiah (1 Kings 22)	Associated with:	King(s):
Nathan (2 Samuel 7—1 Kings 1)	Associated with:	King(s):

VI. The apostles

A. The word apostle means _____. In fact, Christ was called _____ (Hebrews 3:1). Why do you think He was given this description? _____

B. The twelve men trained and sent by Christ were to do what work? _____

C. In the space of one generation, what did Paul say had happened **(Colossians 1:5-6, 23)**? _____

D. Name some things these men suffered for the cause of Christ. _____

VII. The early preachers and teachers

    A. In the first century, we find that almost every Christian had their part in teaching others the gospel.

    B. What contribution did the following people make in the spreading of the gospel?

        1. Ananias **(Acts 9)** _____

        2. Aquila and Priscilla **(Acts 18:24-28; Romans 16:3-5)** _____

        3. Philip **(Acts 8, 21:8)** _____

        4. Lois and Eunice **(Acts 16:1-2; II Timothy 1:5, 3:15)** _____

ASSIGNMENTS

(Hint: Assignments increase in difficulty. While you may not be able to answer each question, please challenge yourself and do the best you can!)

1. Do you know the books of the Bible? (You should know **Genesis—Amos**. Memorize the next 10 books of the Bible.) Do you know the judges? Do you know the sons of Israel?

2. Look at your lesson again. Which characters in our study are found in the Old Testament? In the New Testament? _____

LESSON 4 Keys to Proper Division in the Bible (Part 1)

3. Choose from the following prophets **(Isaiah; Ezekiel; Malachi; Micah; Zechariah)** and name a Messianic prophecy proclaimed.

   a. Show how that prophecy was fulfilled in Christ. _____
   _____
   _____
   _____

   b. Extra credit: Choose a prophecy from all the other prophets and do the same. _____
   _____
   _____
   _____
   _____
   _____
   _____
   _____
   _____
   _____
   _____

4. Name the apostle

   a. Whom Jesus loved _____

   b. Born out of due time _____

   c. Named by Chist (Cephas) _____

   d. Who was a tax collector _____

   e. Who was a Zealot (a sect of the Jews) _____

Lesson 5

Keys to Proper Division in the Bible (Part 2)

INTRODUCTION

I. MEMORY VERSE: **Romans 15:4; John 5:39**

II. This lesson focuses on Christ the Lord and how He is the key figure in the Bible.

III. Truly it is amazing to consider how much of the Bible (Old and New Testament) points to Christ.

    A. In the Old Testament, we see people, teachings, and events pointing _____ Christ.

    B. In the New Testament, we see people, teachings, and events pointing _____ Christ.

IV. Why should we study about Christ in this way?

    A. Because He is the Son of God.

    B. Because He is our Savior and Redeemer.

    C. Because the theme of the Bible is _____, and He made it a reality.

    D. Because one cannot read the Bible without being impressed with the emphasis placed upon Christ.

V. Seeing Christ in the Scriptures helps us to rightly divide the word of God. Please consider the list below with its applications, and understand that this is just a sampling of Scriptures.

DISCUSSION

I. The life of Christ

    A. Christ came into this world, born of a woman named _____. Christ's earthly father was _____. Joseph is described as: _____ **(Matthew 1:19)**.

    1. They also were concerned parents, as they sought Jesus (age 12) for _____ after they lost Him when they left Jerusalem **(Luke 2:41-49)**.
    2. Mary was even found at _____ as Christ was crucified **(John 19:25)**.
  B. Christ's purpose in coming to this earth was _____ **(Luke 19:10)**.
    1. Jesus also told Pilate, _____ **(John 18:37)**.
    2. Paul made a similar statement to Luke when he wrote to Timothy **(1 Timothy 1:15)**.
  C. Christ died, was buried and arose. Why did these things happen?
    ❏ by accident (Jesus was a victim of circumstance) OR
    ❏ as a fulfillment of the Word of God.
    (Hint: **1 Corinthians 15:1-4**)
    1. Read **Romans 6:3-4, 17-18**. What is the action we take that follows the pattern of Christ's death, burial and resurrection? _____
    2. In Christ's death, He purchased _____ **(Acts 20:28)**.
  D. Christ's life is said to be our _____ **(1 Peter 2:21-22)**.
  E. Since Christ died for us, we need to _____ **(2 Corinthians 5:14-15)**.
II. The great emphasis placed on Christ in the Old and New Testament
  A. Please take some time to read and study the background behind the following characters and events:
    1. Adam **(Genesis 2-3)**
    2. Abraham and Isaac (ex: the sacrifice of Isaac, **Genesis 22:1-14**)
    3. Moses (some aspects of his life and character and the Passover in **Exodus 12**)
    4. The judges (What does judge mean?)
    5. The prophets (What does prophet mean? Think about how Christ could be compared to Elijah and Jeremiah.)

LESSON 5 Keys to Proper Division in the Bible (Part 2)

B. How do these people relate to Christ? Turn to the New Testament and see:

1. Adam

   a. Paul calls Adam the figure of _____ **(Romans 5:14)**.

   b. Paul calls Adam _____ **(1 Corinthians 15:45, 47)**.

   c. Paul calls Christ _____ **(1 Corinthians 15:45, 47)**.

   d. Though Adam is called living, Christ is called _____.

2. Abraham and Isaac

   a. On the mountain, there is a spiritual truth that would happen many years in the future **(Genesis 22:1-14)**. See also **John 3:16**.

   b. In Abraham, we see a picture of _____. In Isaac we see a picture of _____.

   c. The difference would be that in the case of Abraham and Isaac, a ram was presented and offered instead of Isaac. In the case of Christ, *he was the lamb offered* **(John 1:29, 36)**!

3. Moses

   a. Name some similarities between Moses and Christ's infancy. _____
   _____
   _____

   b. Yet, the Holy Spirit shows us that _____ was better than _____ **(Hebrews 3:1-6)**.

   c. Moses was considered a _____ in the house, while Christ was called a _____ in the house.

   d. Christ is called our Passover (_____). Why? _____
   _____
   _____

4. The judges

   a. What does the word judge mean? _____

   b. In what way would this apply to Christ? _____
   _____

5. The prophets
   a. What does the word prophet mean? _____
   _____

   b. Why might Christ be compared to Elijah or Jeremiah **(Matthew 16:14)**? _____
   _____

   c. In fact, Jesus was called a prophet **(Deuteronomy 18:15, 18; Acts 3:23-24)**.

C. We can never look at Old Testament people, places, and events in the same way again. Each one points us to Christ!

ASSIGNMENTS

(Hint: Assignments increase in difficulty. While you may not be able to answer each question, please challenge yourself and do the best you can!)

1. Do you know the books of the Bible? (You should know **Genesis—Matthew**. Memorize the next 10 books of the Bible.)

2. Do you know the apostles? Do you know the sons of Israel? Do you know the judges?

3. Read and study **Matthew 16:18**. Be prepared to explain this passage as if you're explaining it to someone for the first time. (Hint: Remember context, remember making applications to someone today, and feel free to use additional verses to explain this text.) _____
_____
_____
_____
_____

Keys to a Good Prayer Life

Lesson 6

INTRODUCTION

I. MEMORY VERSE: **1 Thessalonians 5:17**

II. No study of Bible basics would be complete without a study of prayer.

  A. Why is this so? It is because our lives as Christians demand communication with God.

  B. Prayer is one of the greatest blessings a Christian has in this life. When one prays, he is talking to God, and God is listening to him.

   1. God speaks to us through _____ **(Romans 10:17; 1 Peter 4:11)**.

   2. We speak to God through prayer.

  C. Just as no earthly relationship can be healthy without open, continued communication, so also our spiritual relationship with God cannot be healthy without communication.

  D. God wants us to speak to Him. God wants us to pour out our hearts to Him. God wants us to lean on Him. Let us have the humility to do so.

III. Let us study the subject of prayer and take time to pray often.

DISCUSSION

I. Prayer in the Old Testament

  A. The first time we read of a prayer being offered to God is when God told _____ to have _____ pray for him that he might live **(Genesis 20:7)**.

   1. On this occasion, _____ was called a prophet as well! (Remember lesson 4 and the study of the word prophet.)

   2. Was the prayer offered? _____ **(Genesis 20:17)**.

   3. This is an example of an intercessory prayer. One was praying on behalf of another for their well-being. **Numbers 11:2** and **21:7** are other examples of intercessory prayer.

B. Obviously, Abraham had a good influence upon those in his household, because the second prayer we read in the Bible is a prayer requesting assistance of God.

1. This prayer was prayed by _____. What was the reason he was praying this prayer **(Genesis 24:12-14)**? _____
_____

2. Another prayer of this type was prayed by _____ when he asked God to deliver him from _____ **(Genesis 32:9-12)**.

C. Gideon, the judge, prayed to God asking for two signs to prove he was the one God had chosen to deliver the people from Midian **(Judges 6:36-40)**. What were the two signs? _____
_____

D. Hannah prayed to have _____ **(1 Samuel 1)**.

E. King Hezekiah prayed to God for protection from enemies **(Isaiah 37:14-20)**. After receiving a threatening letter from the Assyrian general, he went _____, spread the letter before the Lord and prayed about it.

F. In captivity, Daniel prayed:

1. For God's help in interpreting the king's dream **(Daniel 2:17-23)**

2. In a consistent manner, _____ daily as he had always done **(Daniel 6:10)**.

3. Confessing his sins and the sins of the nation, praising the greatness of God, and asking for forgiveness **(Daniel 9:4-19)**.

G. Nehemiah prayed for restoration/rebuilding of Jerusalem's walls **(Nehemiah 1:4-11)** and before making his request to the king **(Nehemiah 2:4)**.

II. Prayer in the New Testament

A. In the New Testament, we read about several characters who are known for prayer. Also, we find that God's people are encouraged to pray on several occasions. In fact, in the New Testament, it is assumed that the Christian is doing this anyway **(Philippians 4:6)**.

LESSON 6 Keys to a Good Prayer Life   33

B. Some noted for their praying:
    1. Jesus
        a. Prayed early: He prayed to God _____ _____ **(Mark 1:35)**.
        b. After feeding the 5,000: He went to a _____ to pray **(Mark 6:46)**.
        c. Prayed before He chose the apostles, i.e., making major decisions **(Luke 6:12)**.
        d. Prayed before His trial and crucifixion
            (_____).
    2. The apostles
        a. The apostles made it clear that their time was needed for _____ and _____ when they had seven men appointed to see to the Grecian widows' needs **(Acts 6:1-4)**.
        b. Paul made mention of his prayers he offered for the brethren in the different congregations.
            i. Paul prayed for the salvation of folks **(Romans 10:1-2)**.
            ii. Paul mentioned two specific prayers offered for the Ephesians:
                1. For their _____ **(1:16-18)**.
                2. For their _____ **(3:14-19)**.
            iii. Paul mentioned his prayers for the Philippians, Colossians, Corinthians, etc.
    3. Early Christians
        a. **Acts 4:24-31** is a prayer to God for _____ _____.
        b. **Acts 12:5** describes prayers of the saints offered on behalf of _____.

C. In the New Testament, the writers encouraged people to pray, and then asked for them to pray for certain things.

1. Pray for _____
   (James 5:15-16; Hebrews 13:18; 2 Thessalonians 3:1).
2. Pray that _____ might be spread (2 Thessalonians 3:1).
3. Pray to God and ask _____ (Acts 8:22-24).
4. Pray to God when _____ (James 5:13).

D. In all of this, we are encouraged to pray on a continual basis **(1 Thessalonians 5:17).**

1. What has **Ephesians 6:18** to do with this discussion of prayer? _____
   _____

2. Sadly, prayer is a neglected part of a Christian's life. How sad this is when we know that prayer does so much **(James 5:16).**
   "The _____ fervent _____ of a _____ _____ availeth _____."

ASSIGNMENTS

(Hint: Assignments increase in difficulty. While you may not be able to answer each question, please challenge yourself and do the best you can!)

1. Do you know the books of the Bible? (You should know **Genesis—Philippians**. Memorize the next 10 books of the Bible.)

2. Name some different types of prayers we find in the Bible. _____
   _____
   _____
   _____

3. Can you name the Old Testament prophet whom God told NOT to pray for the people? _____ In fact, God told this prophet not to pray a total of _____ times!

4. Name some people who are known for praying. What characteristics do these people show? _____
   _____
   _____
   _____

Lesson 7

Keynotes of Scripture (Part 1)

INTRODUCTION

I. MEMORY VERSE: **Psalm 119:104**

II. In music, each composition has its keynote. Keynote is defined as the note or tone on which a key or system of tones is founded (*Webster's*).

　A. The beautiful melody and harmony being heard in a musical composition come as a result of the work being founded or centered on the keynote (A, C, B flat, etc.).

　B. In like manner, the Bible has a keynote, _____ , and each book of the Bible corresponds with its own keynote, which produces a beautiful harmony of doctrine and insight into the mind of God, when respected!

III. Each keynote can sum up in a word or two the content of the entire book.

IV. In this and the following two lessons, we will study the keynotes of Scripture. Note that our purpose is to study the keynotes rather than have an in-depth study of each book. I hope that these studies ignite an interest in deeper study of each book of the Bible.

DISCUSSION

I. Genesis

　A. Keynote: Beginnings or origins

　B. In this book we read of the beginnings of _____
　　_____

　C. This book even declares the beginnings of Messianic prophecy **(Genesis 3:15, 12:3, 49:10)**.

II. Exodus

　A. Keynote: Passover

　B. To what does this term refer? _____
　　_____

1. In what chapter do we read about the Passover? _____
2. Was this not the central event of Exodus? _____ Was this not the climax to the ten plagues? _____
   a. All chapters before this point toward the people's redemption and escape (examples: God choosing a leader, the plagues, etc.); the chapters after this (the journey, giving of the Law, etc.) can only happen because of the Lord passing over and their escape.
   b. What do the people do to ensure the Lord passed over them? _____

III. Leviticus
   A. Keynote: Sanctification or holiness
      1. The word holy is found 94 times in this book.
      2. Question: How can sinful man be holy before God? This book is written to tell those men and women of the Old Testament what is necessary to be holy.
   B. The book of Leviticus is filled with sacrifices, washings, sprinkling with blood, etc. These all point to the fact that God's people are to be holy and special people.

IV. Numbers
   A. Keynote: Journey
      1. The book of Numbers condenses some 40 years of Israelite history into a readable book of Bible history **(Numbers 33:1-2)**.
      2. This book reveals the second observance of the Passover since they left Egypt (_____) as well as the journey the people made from _____ to _____.
      3. We then read of their wandering in the wilderness after they rebelled against God.
   B. The journey of these people, their temptations, victories, and defeats mirror what people face today.

V. Deuteronomy
   A. Keynote: Obedience

LESSON 7 Keynotes of Scripture (Part 1)   37

B. The Jews call this book *Mishneh Hattorah* (Repetition of the Law).

1. Within this book, we read where Moses repeats the Ten Commandments (_____).

2. The emphasis on obedience continues throughout the book.

   a. What doth the Lord thy God require of thee **(Deuteronomy 10:12-13)?** _____
   _____
   _____
   _____

   b. Remember the ceremony they are told to perform at Mounts Gerizim and Ebal **(Deuteronomy 27-28)?**

   c. How did this ceremony reflect the theme of obedience in this book?
   _____
   _____

VI. Joshua

   A. Keynote: Possession

   B. In this book, we read where the Israelites finally get to take possession of the land that had originally been promised to _____ .

   1. Not only is this book about possession, but *total* possession of the land that was promised.

   2. **Joshua 21:43-45, 23:14**

   C. Like the book of Numbers, we are shown people who make mistakes by rebellion and sinning in other ways. Yet God is faithful, honoring His promise!

VII. Judges

   A. Keynote: Government

   1. In our study, we see the latter end of the book emphasizing the *lack* of government **(Judges 17:6, 18:1, 19:1, 21:25).**

   2. The judges of the Old Testament have more responsibilities than simply deciding differences between people.

      a. They are military leaders, delivering Israel from the enemies (Moab, Midian, Philistines, etc.).

b. They govern the people once they are delivered and at peace.

B. The judges keep the people in line while they lived, but sadly, at the death of the judge, _____.

C. A good overview for the cycle of 300 years of judges is found in **Judges 2:14-19**.

ASSIGNMENTS

(These assignments are a little different this week. After question #1, each question directly relates to the points made in this lesson.)

1. Do you know the books of the Bible? (You should know **Genesis—1 Peter**. Memorize the rest of the New Testament.)
2. Who is responsible for our origins/beginnings **(John 1:1-13; Colossians 1:15-17)**? _____
3. Who is called our Passover today and why? _____
4. Who is it that makes men holy today and how? _____
5. Who is it that was lifted up like the brass serpent was lifted up? _____
6. Joshua (a Hebrew name) has a Greek equivalent: _____
7. Judge (or, "deliverer") was a foreshadowing of _____.
8. Memorize the keynotes we have studied in this lesson. Lord willing, we will talk about more keynotes in our next lesson.

Lesson 8

Keynotes of Scripture (Part 2)

INTRODUCTION

I. MEMORY VERSE: **Psalm 119:93**

II. This lesson continues the study of the keynotes of Scripture. Make sure to review the last lesson in conjunction with this study.

DISCUSSION

I. Ruth

   A. Keynote: Redemption

   B. Ruth's mother-in-law is _____. After having been widowed, they return to _____ to live **(Ruth 1:2, 7-19)**.

   1. After a series of events, Ruth meets a man named _____ **(Ruth 2:1-3)**, who is willing to redeem her and the property owned by _____.

   2. What is the practice for redeeming property? _____ _____ **(Ruth 4:7-9)**.

   C. Spiritual redemption is alluded to in this book, when we learn Ruth is a part of the lineage leading to Christ. Name the descendants of Ruth mentioned in this book. What relation is she to Jesse? To David? _____ _____

II. Samuel

   A. Keynote: Kingdom

   1. Originally, 1 and 2 Samuel were only known as Samuel. I have combined these two books in this study because both books have the same keynote.

   2. 1 and 2 Samuel record for us the end of one era and the beginning of another. In 1 Samuel, the era of the _____ is ending, and the era of _____ is beginning.

B. Is Israel's demand for a king totally unforeseen by God? _____

C. Some Messianic prophecies in 1 and 2 Samuel:

1. **1 Samuel 2:9-10**: Even before Israel had an earthly king, Hannah spoke of a king. Man's strength cannot prevail over God, for He breaks the adversaries in pieces! God gives strength to *His* king! Ultimately, this has reference to _____.

2. **2 Samuel 7:12-14**: "And when thy days be fulfilled, and thou shalt sleep with thy fathers, I will _____ _____ thy _____ after thee, which shall proceed out of thy bowels, and I will _____ his _____. He shall build an _____ for my _____, and I will _____ the throne of his _____ for ever. I will be his _____, and he shall be my _____..."

3. While there is something to be said concerning Solomon fulfilling this role, ultimately it is Christ who fulfilled this prophecy. Peter and the apostles say this in **Acts 2:29-30**.

III. Kings

A. Keynote: Royalty

B. These two books record the history of God's people beginning with the United Kingdom, ruled by _____, _____, and _____; then dividing into two kingdoms (_____ and _____), until Jerusalem is finally destroyed and the Temple burned down by the _____ in **2 Kings 25**.

1. These two books record the people's continual and gradual rejection of God until they are finally removed by God. These books focus primarily on the kings of Israel.

2. Like the judges, we find the people still caught in the same cycle of righteousness and wickedness. In these books, we see that the people's actions depend largely upon who is ruling. If a righteous king ruled, _____, but if a wicked king ruled, _____.

IV. Chronicles

A. Keynote: Theocracy

LESSON 8 Keynotes of Scripture (Part 2)

1. In the Chronicles (as well as in Kings) we are constantly reminded that the Israelite nation was a theocracy. The king is never mentioned without also mentioning _____.

2. Name some of the prophets that lived during this time period. _____
_____
_____

B. The Chronicles of the Jews are certainly worthy of our study. Though often the events, people, and places mentioned in these volumes are similar to what was stated in Samuel or Kings, these books give us greater insight into the people's lives.

1. The Chronicles begin with _____ and trace the Israelites' history until the final destruction of _____.

2. The Chronicles primarily focus on the kings of Judah. In order to get the full picture of the Divided Kingdom, you need to read both Kings and Chronicles.

V. Ezra—Nehemiah

A. Keynote: Restoration

B. Ezra's name means "help" or "my helper." This is significant when we realize that Ezra is a help to _____. This help came in the form of:

1. Getting these people to finish the work on the Temple: This complemented the work of the prophets _____ and _____ who had already spoken to the people **(Ezra 5:1)**.

2. Pointing the people back to God **(Ezra 7:6, 10)**.

3. Crying out and praying on behalf of the people that God might forgive their sins **(Ezra 9:5-15)**.

4. Encouraging the people to get out of those marriages which were not lawful **(Ezra 10:1-3, 9-14)**.

C. While Ezra is helping the people rebuild the Temple, Nehemiah is organizing people to rebuild _____.

1. This book records the struggles and victories of God's people as they did this work.

2. At this time the book of God was read, and they were encouraged to return to do just what God has said **(Nehemiah 8)**.

ASSIGNMENTS

(These assignments are a little different this week. After question #1, each question directly relates to the points made in this lesson.)

1. Do you know *all* the books of the Bible? Do you know the sons of Israel? Do you know the Judges?

2. Ruth's place in the Bible's theme of redemption is seen: _____
   _____.
   She is only named once in the New Testament and is one of four women to be mentioned in connection with the Lord's lineage **(Matthew 1:3, 5, 6)**.

3. In 2 Samuel, we see that it is through the King _____ that the King of Kings is born (See also: **Matthew 1:6-7**).

   a. **2 Samuel 7:14** sees its fulfillment in Christ, as is explained in **Hebrews 1:5**.

4. Name some of the Messianic prophets present in the days of the Kings. _____
   _____

5. Ezra is a help to the returning Jews. Who is our help today **(Hebrews 4:16, 13:6)**?
   _____

   a. Who is our leader? _____

   b. Who is the remnant today? _____

   c. Who is it that makes intercession for us and our sins **(Hebrews 7:25; 1 John 2:1)**? _____

   d. Who is it that calls men and women to repentance **(Matthew 9:13; Acts 5:31; 2 Peter 3:9)**? _____

Lesson 9

Keynotes of Scripture (Part 3)

INTRODUCTION

I. MEMORY VERSE: **Psalm 119:97**

II. This lesson brings the study of the keynotes of Scripture to a close, as well as this Bible study.

DISCUSSION

I. Esther

   A. Keynote: Providence

      1. Within this book, there is intrigue, betrayal, attempted murder, conspiracy, along with love, faith, courage, and justice. This book also has a happy ending.

      2. Name some of the main characters in this book._____
      _____

      3. While the hand of God is seen on almost every page, _____ is never mentioned in the book!

   B. The pivotal chapter in this book is **Esther 4**. Explain what happens here:
      _____
      _____
      _____
      _____.

   C. Thanks to God's providence, the Jews are spared from certain death, and Haman is executed.

II. Job—Song of Solomon

   A. Keynote: Wisdom

   B. Each book in its own way contrasts the wisdom of God with the wisdom of men.

      1. In Job, there are times when godly people suffer hardships, even though they have done nothing to deserve it. The wisdom of God is seen in the

last few chapters of Job when God speaks to Job about creation and the world He controls.

2. In Psalms, probably the most obvious example of wisdom is **Psalm 119**, where David said he was _____ than _____ because he _____ **(v. 98-100)**.

3. Proverbs speaks freely of God's wisdom, declaring how wisdom cries out to foolish men **(Proverbs 8:1-4)**. Solomon speaks as a father to a son, stating the necessity of getting wisdom. The _____ man is the one who gets wisdom **(Proverbs 3:13)**.

4. While Ecclesiastes deals primarily with life under the sun (a phrase used 29 times), the conclusion of the book (and of life) is what interests us: _____

5. Song of Solomon confuses some, but put simply, it is a book recording the love a husband has for a wife. Most suggest that it is the love Solomon himself has for his bride.

   a. From this, the spiritual application has been made that this book reflects the pure love Christ (groom/husband) has for His church (bride/wife). See also **Ephesians 5:22-33**.

   b. Wisdom is seen in God's plan for marriage (one man and one woman for life). We also see wisdom when we consider Christ and the church, which was in God's mind from eternity **(Ephesians 3:10-11)**.

III. Major and minor prophets

   A. Keynote: Deliverance

   B. The keynote of deliverance (physical and spiritual) is seen in every prophetic book.

   1. Prophets from various backgrounds cried out against people's sins, calling for them to return to the Lord. Prophets cried out for the people to repent so that God would bless them.

   2. They continued to preach and warn until God sent the heathen nations to punish them (examples: **Ezekiel, Jeremiah**, etc.).

   3. After this, the people's repentance was required so that God would spare the remnant and they could return to their homeland (examples: **Isaiah 10:21-22, 35:3-10; Jeremiah 24, 29:1-10**; etc.).

4. At the same time, through these prophets, God promised a Savior that would come in the future (**Isaiah 7:14, 9:6, 11:1, 53; Daniel 7:13-14; Ezekiel 21:24-27**; etc.).

5. Many of the major and minor prophets were quoted by Jesus and the apostles.

IV. The Gospel records and Acts

   A. Keynote: Christ has come

   1. The four gospel records proclaim Christ has come (**Matthew 1:23, 2:1, 16:16**; etc.). They record the life of Christ on earth, His death, burial, and resurrection for the remission of man's sin.

   2. The book of Acts points one back to those times, saying Christ has come to earth and has returned to Heaven (**Acts 13:29-31, 17:18, 31**; etc.).

   B. The book of Acts records the eyewitness testimonies from people who saw Jesus, heard Him speak, and followed His will (examples: **1 John 1:1; 2 Peter 1:16; Acts 1:3**).

V. Epistles

   A. Keynote: Faithfulness to Christ

   B. The 21 epistles (to churches and individuals) speak to the responsibility each one has as a result of being redeemed from sin because of Christ and His sacrifice.

VI. Revelation

   A. Keynote: Victory in Christ, or overcoming with Christ **(Revelation 17:14)**

   B. The book of Revelation confuses many because they wish to interpret this book in light of what they see in current events. This is a mistake!

   1. A well-grounded and strong foundation in the writings of the Old Testament is what is necessary for understanding this book.

   2. This book is written to the seven churches in Asia **(Revelation 1:4, 11)**, and points them (and us) to victory in Christ.

   3. The called, chosen, and faithful will overcome with the Lamb **(Revelation 17:14)**. Who are the called, chosen, and faithful? It is those who have been redeemed by the blood of Christ **(Revelation 1:5)**.

ASSIGNMENTS

(These assignments are a little different this week. After question #2, each question directly relates to the points made in this lesson.)

1. Do you know *all* the books of the Bible? Do you know the sons of Israel? Do you know the Judges? Do you know the apostles?

2. Do you remember some of the keynotes from previous books studied?

3. Can we see God's providence in the life of our Savior? _____
   Name some examples. _____
   _____
   _____
   _____

4. In light of Job—Song of Solomon, consider Paul's words in **1 Corinthians 1:18-31**. Paul said God's wisdom surpasses _____

5. Name some major and minor prophets quoted by Jesus and the apostles. _____
   _____
   _____
   _____

6. What is the value of reading eyewitness testimony concerning an event? How many writers in the New Testament saw Christ before, during, or after His resurrection? _____ How many did Paul say saw Christ after His resurrection **(1 Corinthians 15:5-8)**? _____

7. Name some churches Paul wrote to whose beginnings are recorded in the book of Acts. _____
   _____
   _____

FINAL THOUGHT

I hope these lessons are helpful in building you up in the faith and increasing your familiarity with the Bible as a whole. May God bless you as you strive to serve Him daily!

www.ingramcontent.com/pod-product-compliance
Lightning Source LLC
Chambersburg PA
CBHW080943040426
42444CB00015B/3428